## Level One

# · gentle ·
# GRAMMAR

An Adaptation of New Language Exercises for Primary Schools
by C. C. Long

ISBN-13: 978-1720816324

ISBN-10: 1720816328

Visit: momdelights.com

# ·PREFACE·

(Excerpted and adapted from the original book.)

These exercises are based upon these principles:

1. That the child learns by example and practice: not by rules or theory.

2. That the habits of utterance which a child begins to form at the very outset will cling to him through life.

He should, therefore, before bad habits of speech and writing are formed, begin with the facts that lead up to general grammatical laws; not as ordinary textbooks require, with rules and definitions.

No examples of false syntax are given, because, so far as possible, we should not allow pupils to see or hear what is wrong in language. The children's mistakes in speaking and writing will be found ample for correction and illustration.

These exercises have been used in large graded schools with the most satisfactory results, and are now offered to teachers with the hope that they may be found useful in leading the "little ones" to correct expression of their thoughts in speaking and writing.

FIRST READER GRADE. — Language culture in this grade should be largely oral. Pictures placed before the pupils, or subjects familiar to them will furnish topics. By a little skillful questioning, pupils may be led to invent a good story founded upon what they see in a picture, or have observed at home, at play, or at school.

# Introduction

## And Instructions

*I* have observed that, **if not corrected early-on, some habits of poor grammar and spelling can become like permanent marker on the walls of a young child's mind.** Even though I agree heartily with the idea that children learn spelling and grammar best by reading and writing, my own children have needed more specific instruction. However, I'm not willing to overburden them with the failed system of presenting a complete English program in every grade. This repeating of the same information year-after-year kills the love of language in children.

**For years I searched for a program that was:**

- **Something I could put on "auto pilot"**

- **Quick (for kids who already had trouble sitting still for reading and math)**

- **Not technical**

**Cheap and easy to put together (not too much printing, cutting, pasting, etc., etc., etc.)**

Early-on I discovered *Simply Grammar,* an expanded version of Charlotte Mason's *First Grammar Lessons.* However, the work was meant to be done orally, which was too much work for a woman juggling children at six different levels at the same time.

Finally, I stumbled upon Dollar Homeschool in *The Old Schoolhouse* magazine. This company specializes in collecting school books from times past and making them available in digital form for modern use. These materials were written before the Progressive education movement in America, a time before humanism and its psychobabble began to rule the way children were taught.

Included on one of the CD's from Dollar Homeschool was a collection of grammar books, and in particular two which I found very interesting. These were written by a person by the name of C. C. Long and were entitled *New Language Exercises for Primary Schools* part one and part two (I like to refer to them as "Long's Language"). **As I read through them I became more and more excited; this was finally the answer, the tool that would help fill the gap and turn my beginning readers into confident, competent writers!**

**For one thing, the first lessons are not about nouns and verbs.** There is actually very little mentioned in the first book about grammar at all, although grammar is the subject. Instead, children are asked to write about themselves, where they live, etc. The lessons present sentences as "statements" including a subject and a predicate without ever mentioning the technical terms. Within the first 50 lessons, my little ones have been able to write short paragraphs that describe familiar objects such as a ball, a cow, etc.

**For another thing, the lessons are oh, so short!** The instructions are usually one or two sentences long, and the exercise is not more than six to twelve short sentences (that follow a formula, so there is not that much thinking involved). If a child is focused, which is easy to do because of the simplicity, the longest lesson takes less than 15 minutes to complete!

**Besides all this, the work is mostly self-directed.** The learning is gradual, no great leaps are expected from one day to another, so little instruction or oversight is necessary. This is certainly a win/win for us moms of many! My children come away from the lessons feeling accomplished and energized without feeling frustrated. Before I realize it they are well on their way to being successful writers!

After I published a post on my blog recommending this resource, I realized there was a way to make things even easier (both for me and for my readers).

**So, I finally sat down with some computer software and began the process of taking the original book and re-engineering it for modern use.**

**The result is what you see here.** As an answer to prayer, I was able to come up with a way that streamlined the lessons and created a worktext of sorts, with the original directions and copywork presented with places directly adjoining for the child to complete the work. The instructions are included in each page — **no extra searching, no lugging around a teacher's manual, no loss due to distraction between the printed page and the actual work.**

**While I tried to keep to the flavor of the original work, I did tweak the lessons in a few areas,** including some correction where the wording was a bit too archaic. I also restructured some of the composition lessons and even wrote a few to add that were more appropriate where necessary.

You will probably want to spend a minute or two on each lesson just to make sure the instructions are understood, and I would also be sure to check up on the lessons to make sure they are done with neatness (remember, a little done well is better than a lot done poorly).

**Easy as pie, right?**

**Please note:** This level is for children who are reading whole words and sentences pretty well. If your child can read an entire Dr. Seuss book pretty easily, he's probably ready.

**Blessings,**

*Sherry*

**P.S. For any further information on this or any other of our projects, please visit our site, momdelights.com**

# LANGUAGE EXERCISES
## FIRST READER GRADE

| | NAMES |
|---|---|
| | Lesson 1. — *Copy these statements.* |
| 1. | My name is Charles Jones. |
| | |
| 2. | I am eight years of age. |
| | |
| 3. | I live on Fourth Street. |
| | |
| 4. | I live in the city of Dayton. |
| | |
| 5. | I go to the Third District School. |
| | |
| 6. | Miss Smith is my teacher. |

# LANGUAGE EXERCISES
## FIRST READER GRADE

**NAMES**

Lesson 2.

1. Write your name.

2. Write the name of your homeschool.

3. Of the city in which you live.

4. Write the name of two places.

5. Of three things in your room.

6. Of two things you can wear.

7. Of two things you can eat.

8. Of two of your playmates.

# LANGUAGE EXERCISES
## FIRST READER GRADE

### NAMES

Lesson 3. — *Write answers in* **complete statements** *as in lesson 2.*

1.  What is your name?

    Example: My name is_____.

2.  What is your age?



3.  On what street do you live?



4.  In what city do you live?



5.  To what school do you go?



6.  Who is your teacher?

# LANGUAGE EXERCISES
## FIRST READER GRADE

| | |
|---|---|
| | **"IS" AND "ARE" IN STATEMENTS** |
| | Lesson 4. — *Copy these sentences. Place a period after each.* |
| 1. | The boy is here. |
| | |
| 2. | The boys are here. |
| | |
| 3. | The girl is happy. |
| | |
| 4. | The girls are happy. |
| | |
| | We use *is* when we speak of *one*. We use *are* when we speak of *more* than one. *Fill in the blanks with "is" or "are."* |
| 1. | The bell _____ ringing. |
| | |
| 2. | The cherries _____ripe. |
| | |
| 3. | The apples _____ sweet. |
| | |
| 4. | Our books _____new. |
| | |

# LANGUAGE EXERCISES
## FIRST READER GRADE

Lesson 5. — *Use "is" in statements about:*

1. a notebook

Example: This is a notebook.

2. an apple

3. a book

4. a table

5. a desk

6. a pencil

7. a picture

8. a door

# LANGUAGE EXERCISES
## FIRST READER GRADE

Lesson 5. (continued)

*Use "are" in statements about:*

1. notebooks

2. apples

3. books

4. tables

5. desks

6. pencils

7. pictures

8. doors

# LANGUAGE EXERCISES
## FIRST READER GRADE

### "IS" AND "ARE" IN QUESTIONS

Lesson 6. — *Copy these sentences. Place this mark (?) at the end of each question.*

| | |
|---|---|
| 1. | Is the boy here? |
| 2. | Are the boys here? |
| 3. | Is the girl happy? |
| 4. | Are the girls happy? |

*Doodle here:*

# LANGUAGE EXERCISES
## FIRST READER GRADE

## "IS" AND "ARE" IN QUESTIONS

Lesson 7. — *Fill the blanks with "is" or "are."*

1. The horse _____ black.

2. _____ the horse black?

3. The apple _____ green.

4. _____ the apple green?

5. The boys _____ happy.

6. _____ the boys happy?

7. The baby _____ asleep.

8. _____ the baby asleep?

9. The birds _____ singing.

10. _____ the birds singing?

11. The hen _____ too fat.

12. _____ the hen too fat?

# LANGUAGE EXERCISES
## FIRST READER GRADE

| | |
|---|---|
| | **"IS" AND "ARE"** |
| | Lesson 8. — *Change "is" to "are," or "are" to "is," and write the sentences correctly.* |
| 1. | The pencil is sharp. |
| | Example: The pencils are sharp. |
| 2. | The peach is sweet. |
| | |
| 3. | The lamp is bright. |
| | |
| 4. | The picture is large. |
| | |
| 5. | Are the hats old? |
| | |
| 6. | Are the flowers red? |
| | |
| 7. | Are the dresses new? |
| | |
| 8. | Are the tables broken? |
| | |
| | |

# LANGUAGE EXERCISES
## FIRST READER GRADE

| | |
|---|---|
| | **"IS" AND "ARE"** |
| | Lesson 9. — *Use "is" to ask something about:* |
| 1. | a notebook |
| | Example: Is a notebook helpful? |
| 2. | an apple |
| | |
| 3. | a ruler |
| | |
| 4. | a book |
| | |
| 5. | a desk |
| | |
| 6. | a pencil |
| | |
| 7. | a picture |
| | |
| 8. | a door |
| | |
| | |

# LANGUAGE EXERCISES
## FIRST READER GRADE

### "IS" AND "ARE"

Lesson 10. — Use "are" to ask something about:

| | |
|---|---|
| 1. | notebooks |
| | |
| 2. | desks |
| | |
| 3. | apples |
| | |
| 4. | pencils |
| | |
| 5. | books |
| | |
| 6. | pictures |
| | |
| 7. | doors |
| | |
| 8. | windows |
| | |
| | |

# LANGUAGE EXERCISES
## FIRST READER GRADE

### MEMORY LESSON

Lesson 11. *Copy these lines. Commit them to memory.*

Do your best, your very best,

And do it every day,

Little boys and little girls,

That is the wisest way.

1.

2.

3.

4.

*Doodle space:*

# LANGUAGE EXERCISES
## FIRST READER GRADE

Lesson 12. — *Write these questions. Notice that each one ends with this mark (?).*

1. Do you see a cat and her kitten?

2. Is the cat large and black?

3. Is she sitting on a mat?

4. Is she looking at the kitten?

5. Is the kitten small and black?

6. Is it sitting on a pan?

# LANGUAGE EXERCISES
## FIRST READER GRADE

Lesson 13. — *Think of your cat. Write six questions about it. Use these words in the questions.*

| | |
|---|---|
| cat | catch mice |
| pur | see at night |
| sharp claws | a coat of soft fur |

1.

2.

3.

4.

5.

6.

# LANGUAGE EXERCISES
## FIRST READER GRADE

### "WAS" AND "WERE"

Lesson 14. — *Copy these sentences.*

1. The paper was torn.

2. The papers were torn.

3. A hen was in the barn.

4. Hens were in the barn.

5. Was the bird in the cage?

6. Were the birds in the cage?

We use *was* when we speak of *one*.

We use *were* when we speak of *more than one*.

# LANGUAGE EXERCISES
## FIRST READER GRADE

Lesson 15. — *Fill the blanks with "was" or "were."*

1. The pencil _____ broken.

2. _____ the pencil broken?

3. The book _____ lost.

4. _____ the book lost?

5. The trees _____ very tall.

6. _____ the trees very tall?

7. The man _____ working.

8. _____ the man working?

9. The boys _____ going to dinner.

10. _____ the boys going to dinner?

*Doodle space:*

# LANGUAGE EXERCISES
## FIRST READER GRADE

Lesson 16. — *Change "was" to "were," or "were" to "was," and write correctly.*

1. The egg was in the nest.

2. The cows were in the pond.

3. Were the trees near the house?

4. The bird was in the cage

5. Was the stone in the water?

6. The girl was in the garden.

7. Were the bells ringing?

8. The cloud was very black.

# LANGUAGE EXERCISES
## FIRST READER GRADE

Lesson 17. — *Make statements with these words.*

1. Fruit, the, sweet, is.

2. Are, hot, days, the.

3. Ink, the, black, was.

4. Were, children, the, asleep.

*Ask questions with these words.*

1. Clara, school, is, in.

2. The, good, are, pens.

3. Pretty, the, dolls, were.

4. White, the rabbits, were.

# LANGUAGE EXERCISES
## FIRST READER GRADE

| | |
|---|---|
| | Lesson 18. — *Use "was" or "were" in statements beginning with:* |
| 1. | I |
| | |
| 2. | We |
| | |
| 3. | He |
| | |
| 4. | She |
| | |
| 5. | They |
| | |
| | *Use "was" or "were" in questions with:* |
| 1. | I |
| | |
| 2. | We |
| | |
| 3. | He |
| | |
| 4. | She |
| | |

# LANGUAGE EXERCISES
## FIRST READER GRADE

| | |
|---|---|
| | Lesson 18.  (continued) |
| 5. | They |
| | |
| | **"HAS" AND "HAVE"** |
| | Lesson 19. — *Write these sentences.* |
| 1. | A bird has claws. |
| | |
| 2. | Birds have claws. |
| | |
| 3. | An apple has a stem. |
| | |
| 4. | Apples have stems. |
| | |
| 5. | Does a cow have  horns? |
| | |
| 6. | Do cows have horns? |
| | |
| | We use *has* when  we speak of *one*.<br><br>We use *have* when we speak of *more* than *one*. |
| | |

# LANGUAGE EXERCISES
## FIRST READER GRADE

*Lesson 20.* — *Change "has" to "have," or "have" to "has," and write these sentences correctly.*

1. The book has leaves.

2. The ships have sails.

3. Do the doors have hinges?

4. Does the apple have seeds?

5. Does the boy have a kind sister?

6. The girls have pretty dolls.

*Doodle here:*

# LANGUAGE EXERCISES
## FIRST READER GRADE

Lesson 21. — *Use "is," "are," "was," or "were" in writing statements about:*

1. sky

2. stars

3. sun

4. glass

5. top

6. window

7. houses

8. clouds

# LANGUAGE EXERCISES
## FIRST READER GRADE

Lesson 21. (continued) *Change your statements to questions.*

1. sky

2. stars

3. sun

4, glass

5. top

6. window

7. houses

8. clouds

# LANGUAGE EXERCISES
## FIRST READER GRADE

| | Lesson 22. — *Use "has" or "have" in writing statements about:* |
|---|---|
| 1. | John |
| | |
| 2. | sled |
| | |
| 3. | boy |
| | |
| 4. | men |
| | |
| 5. | girl |
| | |
| 6. | knives |
| | |
| 7. | child |
| | |
| 8. | children |
| | |
| | |
| | |
| | |

# LANGUAGE EXERCISES
## FIRST READER GRADE

| | |
|---|---|
| | Lesson 23. — *Use "has" or "have" in writing statements beginning with:* |
| 1. | I |
| | |
| 2. | We |
| | |
| 3. | He |
| | |
| 4. | She |
| | |
| 5. | They |
| | |
| | *Use "has" or "have" in writing questions with:* |
| 1. | I |
| | |
| 2. | We |
| | |
| 3. | He |
| | |
| 4. | She |
| | |

# LANGUAGE EXERCISES
## FIRST READER GRADE

| | |
|---|---|
| | Lesson 24. — *Words to use with "you."* |
| 1. | Write a statement, using *you* with *are*. |
| | |
| 2. | Write a statement, using *you* with *were*. |
| | |
| 3. | Write a statement, using *you* with *have*. |
| | |
| 4. | Write a question, using *you* with *are*. |
| | |
| 5. | Write a question, using *you* with *were*. |
| | |
| 6. | Write a question, using *you* with *have*. |
| | |
| | *Doodle here:* |

# LANGUAGE EXERCISES
## FIRST READER GRADE

Lesson 25. — *Copy these lines and commit to memory.*

1. Little drops of rain

2.     Bring the springing flowers,

3. And I may attain

4.     Much by little powers.

1.

2.

3.

4.

*Doodle here:*

# LANGUAGE EXERCISES
## FIRST READER GRADE

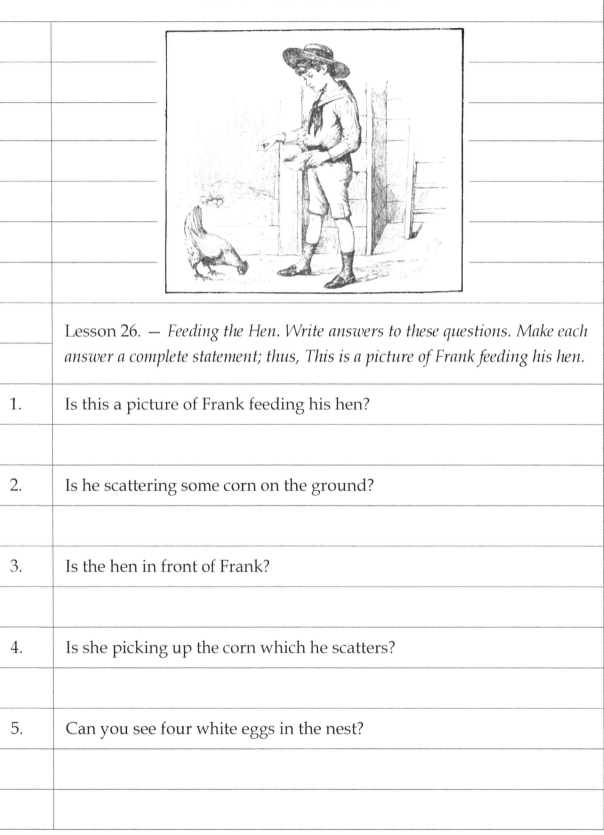

Lesson 26. — *Feeding the Hen. Write answers to these questions. Make each answer a complete statement; thus, This is a picture of Frank feeding his hen.*

| 1. | Is this a picture of Frank feeding his hen? |
|----|----|
|    |    |
| 2. | Is he scattering some corn on the ground? |
|    |    |
| 3. | Is the hen in front of Frank? |
|    |    |
| 4. | Is she picking up the corn which he scatters? |
|    |    |
| 5. | Can you see four white eggs in the nest? |
|    |    |
|    |    |

# LANGUAGE EXERCISES
## FIRST READER GRADE

### NAMES OF THE DAYS.

Lesson 27. — *Copy the names of the days of the week.*

| | |
|---|---|
| 1. | Sunday |
| 2. | Monday |
| 3. | Tuesday |
| 4. | Wednesday |
| 5. | Thursday |
| 6. | Friday |
| 7. | Saturday |

*How many days are there in a week?*

Lesson 28. — *Write seven statements, telling one thing you did on each day of the last week; as,*

I went to church on Sunday.

On Monday I went to school.

I bought a book on Tuesday.

1.

2.

# LANGUAGE EXERCISES
## FIRST READER GRADE

| | |
|---|---|
| | Lesson 28.  (continued) |
| 3. | |
| | |
| 4. | |
| | |
| 5. | |
| | |
| 6. | |
| | |
| 7. | |
| | |

Lesson 29. — *Use one of these words correctly in each of the blanks:  "two," "hear," "to," "here," "too."*

He went _____the window.

The horse is _____ fat to run.

John has _____ hands.

Sarah was _____yesterday.

Did you _____ the bird sing?

# LANGUAGE EXERCISES
## FIRST READER GRADE

Lesson 30. — *Use one of these words correctly in each of the blanks:* "know," "there," "no," "their."

1. They went _____ on Monday.

2. The boys lost _____ slates.

3. Did you come late? _____, I came early.

4. I _____ how much this book costs.

Lesson 31. — *Use one of these words correctly in each of the blanks:* "write," "right," "new," "knew."

1. Tom has a _____ top.

2. Harry _____ his cousin's name.

3. It is not _____ to hurt a dog.

4. Mary and James _____ neatly in their books.

# LANGUAGE EXERCISES
## FIRST READER GRADE

### COLORS.

*TEACHER: Go over the colors red, yellow, and blue.*

Lesson 32.

1. Name two kinds of red fruit.

2. What flower is red.

3. What flower is yellow.

4. Ask a question about a bird that is yellow.

5. Write a statement about something that is black.

6. What is the color of the sky?

# LANGUAGE EXERCISES
## FIRST READER GRADE

Lesson 33.

1. What colors are seen in our flag?

2. Name something we wear, and tell the color.

3. Write a statement about something that is black.

4. Write a statement about something that is white.

*Doodle here:*

# LANGUAGE EXERCISES
## FIRST READER GRADE

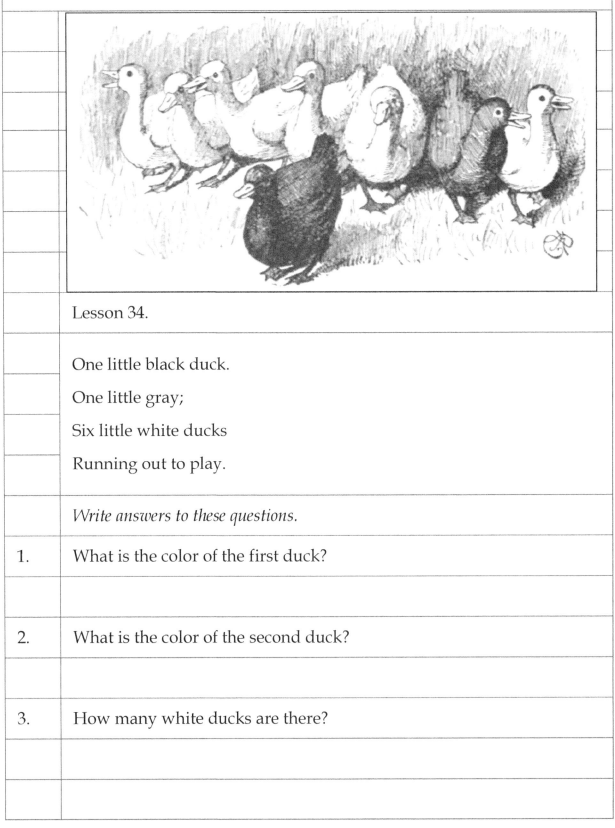

Lesson 34.

One little black duck.

One little gray;

Six little white ducks

Running out to play.

*Write answers to these questions.*

1. What is the color of the first duck?

2. What is the color of the second duck?

3. How many white ducks are there?

# LANGUAGE EXERCISES
## FIRST READER GRADE

| | |
|---|---|
| | Lesson 34.  (continued) |
| 4. | How many ducks in all? |
| | |
| 5. | What are they doing? |
| | |
| | **PARTS OF OBJECTS** |

*TO THE TEACHER.* – *In all cases, present the object and ask the children to point out the parts, or state the qualities.*

| | |
|---|---|
| | Lesson 35. — *Write these sentences.* |
| 1. | The bell has a handle. |
| | |
| 2. | The bell has a clapper. |
| | |
| | *Name two parts of the bell in one sentence.* |
| | The bell has a handle and a clapper. |
| | |
| 1. | A book has a cover. |
| | A book has leaves. |
| | A book has _____ and _____. |
| | |

# LANGUAGE EXERCISES
## FIRST READER GRADE

| | |
|---|---|
| | Lesson 35  (continued) |
| 2. | An apple has pulp. |
| | An apple has seeds. |
| | An apple has _____ and _____. |
| | |
| | Lesson 36. — *Write these sentences.* |
| 1. | A knife has a handle. |
| | A knife has a blade. |
| | A knife has a _____ and _____. |
| | |
| 2. | A hat has a brim. |
| | A hat has a crown. |
| | A hat has a _____ and a _____. |
| | |
| | Lesson 37. — *Write these sentences.* |
| 1. | The paper is thin. |
| | The paper is smooth. |
| | The paper is _____ and _____. |
| | |
| | |

# LANGUAGE EXERCISES
## FIRST READER GRADE

| | |
|---|---|
| | Lesson 37.  (continued) |
| 2. | The lemon is yellow. |
| | The lemon is sour. |
| | The lemon is _____ and _____. |
| | |
| | Lesson 38. |
| 1. | Iron is hard. |
| | Iron is heavy. |
| | *Tell about  iron in one sentence.* |
| | |
| | |
| 2. | Gold is heavy. |
| | Gold is yellow. |
| | *Tell about gold in one sentence.* |
| | |
| | |
| | |
| | |
| | |
| | |

# LANGUAGE EXERCISES
## FIRST READER GRADE

Lesson 39.

| round | sweet | black | clear | soft |
|-------|-------|-------|-------|------|
| white | juicy | hard | smooth | warm |

*Write five statements, telling:*

1. Two qualities of a crayon.

Example: A crayon is hard and smooth.

2. Two qualities of an orange.

3. Two qualities of coal.

4. Two qualities of glass.

5. Two qualities of wool.

# LANGUAGE EXERCISES
## FIRST READER GRADE

Lesson 40. — *Write these sentences.*

1. The apple is round. The orange is round.

The apple and orange _____ _____.

2. Iron is heavy. Gold is heavy.

Iron and gold _____ _____.

Lesson 41.

|        |       |       |       |
|--------|-------|-------|-------|
| iron   | ant   | lion  | glass |
| stone  | fly   | horse | chalk |

*Write four sentences, telling:*

1. What are hard.

2. What are small.

3. What are strong.

4. What are brittle.

# LANGUAGE EXERCISES
## FIRST READER GRADE

Lesson 42. — *Getting the Eggs.*

*Write answers to the questions in complete statements.*

1. What is this girl's name?

2. Where do you think she has been?

3. What did she go there for?

4. What does she hold with both hands?

5. What are in the pan?

6. Where is the little chicken?

# LANGUAGE EXERCISES
## FIRST READER GRADE

*When possible, show the object to the student.*

Lesson 43. — *The Peach.*

1. On what do peaches grow?

2. Of what use are they?

3. What do we call the part we eat?

Lesson 44. *The Knife.*

1. Name two parts of the knife.

2. What part of the knife is sharp?

3. For what do we use the knife?

# LANGUAGE EXERCISES
## FIRST READER GRADE

| | |
|---|---|
| | Lesson 45. — *The Apple.* |
| 1. | What is the color of the apple? |
| | |
| 2. | What is its shape? |
| | |
| 3. | For what is it used? |
| | |
| 4. | On what kind of a tree does it grow? |
| | |
| 5. | How do some apples taste? |
| | |
| | Lesson 46. — *Leather.* |
| 1. | What is leather? |
| | |
| 2. | Can you tear leather? |
| | |
| 3. | Why does leather make good shoes? |
| | |
| 4. | How many uses of leather do you know? |
| | |

# LANGUAGE EXERCISES
## FIRST READER GRADE

Lesson 47. — *The Paper.*

Write a statement about the color of paper. Tell how it feels. In one sentence, state what you have written about paper. For what is paper used?

# LANGUAGE EXERCISES
## FIRST READER GRADE

Lesson 48. — *The Cow. Write complete answers.*

| | |
|---|---|
| 1. | Where have you seen a cow? |
| 2. | What does the cow eat? |
| 3. | What do we get from the cow? |

Lesson 49. — *A Ball.*

| | |
|---|---|
| 1. | What shape is a ball? |
| 2. | Of what is it made? |
| 3. | What can you do with a ball? |

# LANGUAGE EXERCISES
## FIRST READER GRADE

Lesson 50.  — *A Book*

1. What is the name of a book you are reading?

2. What are the parts of a book?

3. What is a book made of?

4. What is a book used for.

5. What does a book cost?

Lesson 51. — *A Boy.*

1. What is the name of a boy you know?

2. Is he a little or a big boy?

3. What color are his eyes?

4. What color is his hair?

# LANGUAGE EXERCISES
## FIRST READER GRADE

Lesson 52. — *My Doll.*

| | |
|---|---|
| 1. | What is its name? |
| | |
| 2. | Is it large or small? |
| | |
| 3. | What color is its hair? |
| | |
| 4. | What kind of clothes does it have on? |
| | |
| 5. | Ask a question about the doll. |
| | |

Lesson 53. — *Homeschool.*

| | |
|---|---|
| 1. | When do you begin? |
| | |
| 2. | How much time does it take? |
| | |
| 3. | What do you read? |
| | |
| 4. | What do you write about? |
| | |

# LANGUAGE EXERCISES
## FIRST READER GRADE

Lesson 54. — *My Notebook.*

1. What is your notebook made of?

2. What color is your notebook?

3. How many pages does it have?

4. What do you write in it?

*Doodle here:*

# LANGUAGE EXERCISES
## FIRST READER GRADE

Lesson 55. — *Write complete answers to the questions.*

1. Do you see May and her pet bird?

2. Do you think she has just fed the bird?

3. What is at the window?

Lesson 56.

May has a pet canary. It was a present from her mother. May calls her bird Danny. It will sit on her hand and sing. The old cat thinks he would like to eat Danny. Will May let the cat get the bird?

Lesson 56.  (continued) *Write a story of May and her bird.*

# LANGUAGE EXERCISES
## FIRST READER GRADE

Lesson 57. — *Write complete answers to the questions.*

1. Do you see the picture of little Lucy?

2. Is Lucy sitting on a large stone?

3. Do her feet hang over the edge of the stone?

4. What is just below her feet?

5. Are her shoes and stockings at her left?

6. Has she a large hat on her head?

7. Do you think Lucy is a good little girl?

# LANGUAGE EXERCISES
## FIRST READER GRADE

Lesson 58.  — *Little Lucy*

1. Was it noon?

2. Was the sun hot?

3. Did she then take off her shoes to cool her feet?

4. Will she soon put both feet in the water?

5. Will Lucy take cold?

6. Will she dry her feet and put on her shoes?

7. Will she then walk to her home?

# LANGUAGE EXERCISES
## FIRST READER GRADE

Lesson 59. — *Write complete answers to the questions.*

1. Is this a picture of Jane and Ella at play?

2. Has Jane light hair?

3. Has Ella dark hair?

4. Where is Jane?

5. What has she in her right hand?

6. Where is Ella?

# LANGUAGE EXERCISES
## FIRST READER GRADE

Lesson 60. — *Write a story about Jane and her doll.*

# LANGUAGE EXERCISES
## FIRST READER GRADE

Lesson 60.  (continued)

# LANGUAGE EXERCISES
## FIRST READER GRADE

Lesson 61. — *Copy and commit these lines.*

| | |
|---|---|
| Little drops of water, | Little deeds of kindness, |
| Little grains of sand, | Little words of love, |
| Make the mighty ocean | Make our earth an Eden, |
| And the pleasant land. | Like the heaven above. |

1.

2.

3.

4.

5.

6.

7.

8.

# LANGUAGE EXERCISES
## FIRST READER GRADE

| | |
|---|---|
| | |
| | |
| | |
| | |
| | |
| | |
| | |
| | |
| | |
| | |
| | |
| | |
| | |
| | |
| | |
| | |
| | |
| | |
| | |

Made in the USA
Monee, IL
31 August 2022

12786731R00037